Oh! My Phonics 1

Alphabet Sounds

CEDU BOOK

INTRODUCTION

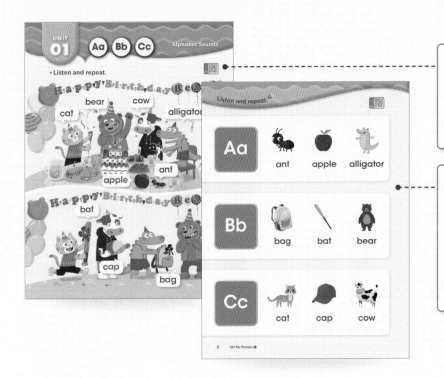

• WORD CHANT

The fun chants and captivating illustrations introduce the target sounds and words.

• LISTEN & REPEAT

Students can learn and practice the target sounds and words. They can also understand the letter-sound relationships.

• WORD READING

Students can practice identifying the target sounds, letters and related words.

• WRITING

The target sounds and letters can be strengthened through writing activities.

• LISTENING

Students can reinforce the target sounds and words through listening activities.

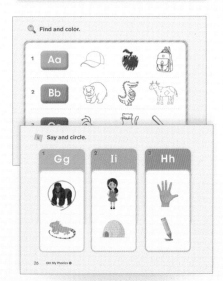

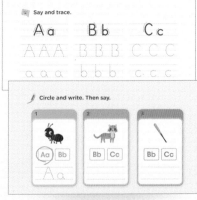

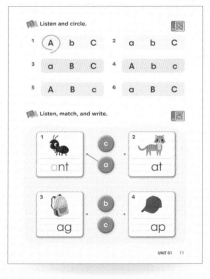

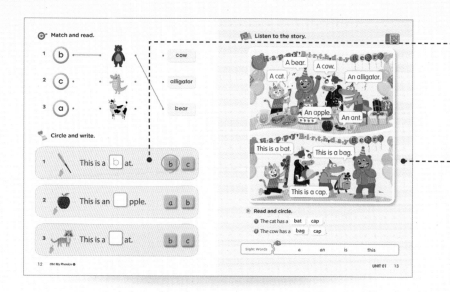

SENTENCE READING

Students can practice reading sentences with the target words.

STORY READING

A phonics story offers students practice with reading target words in natural contexts. They can naturally improve their sight word reading skills.

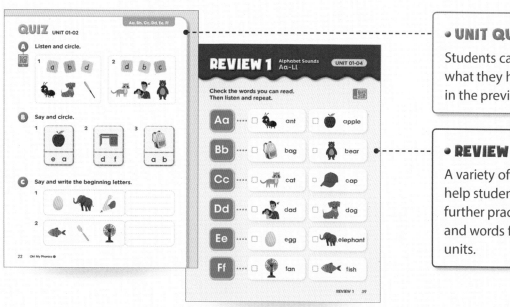

UNIT QUIZ

Students can check what they have learned in the previous two units.

REVIEW

A variety of activities can help students recall and further practice the sounds and words from previous units.

WORKBOOK

Students can reinforce what they have learned by completing the follow-up exercises featured in the accompanying workbook.

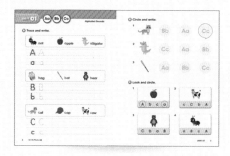

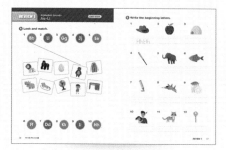

CONTENTS

• **Listen and chant.**

Happy Birthday Bear!

cat

bear

cow

alligator

apple

ant

Happy Birthday Bear!

bat

cap

bag

Aa

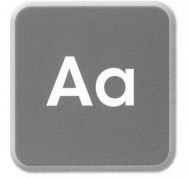

 ant

 apple

 alligator

Bb

 bag

 bat

 bear

Cc

 cat

 cap

 cow

Say and trace.

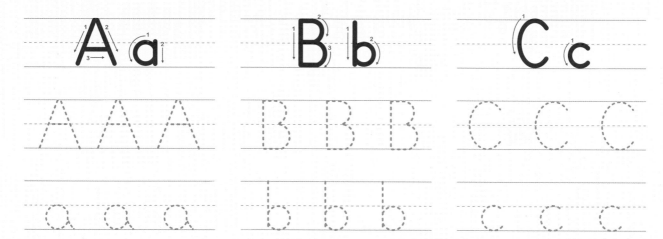

 Listen and circle.

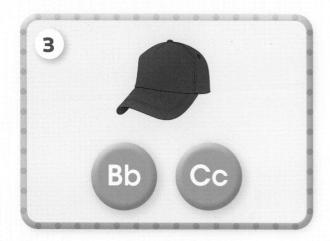

Circle and write. Then say.

1
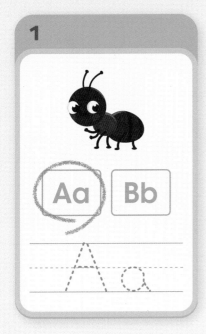

Aa   Bb

Aa

2

Bb   Cc

3
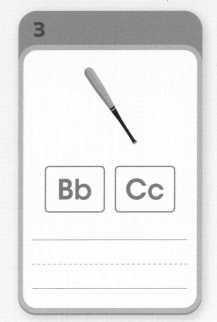

Bb   Cc

 ## Find and color.

1 Aa

2 Bb

3 Cc

Listen and circle.

1 **(A)** b C   2 a b C

3 a B C   4 A b c

5 A B c   6 a B C

 Listen, match, and write.

1 ant

c

a

2 at

3 ag

b

c

4 ap

Match and read.

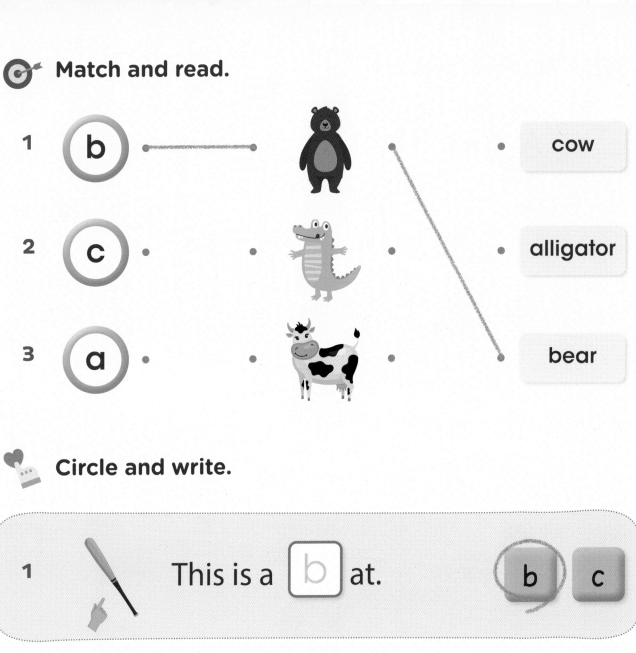

1 b — bear

2 c — cow

3 a — alligator

Circle and write.

1 This is a b at. (b) c

2 This is an ☐ pple. a b

3 This is a ☐ at. b c

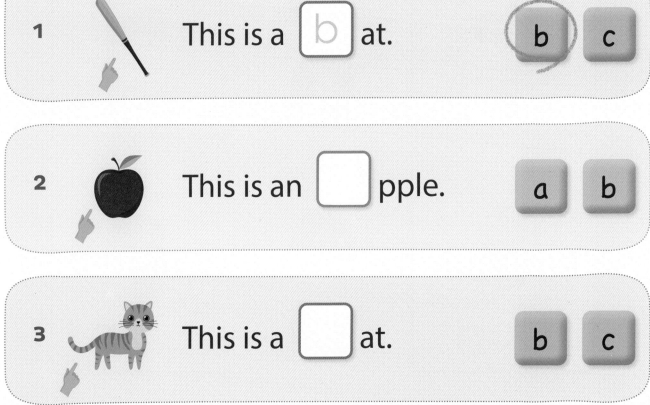

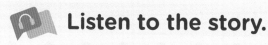

※ **Read and circle.**

1 The cat has a [**bat**   **cap**].

2 The cow has a [**bag**   **cap**].

Sight Words	a	an	is	this

QUIZ UNIT 01

07

A Listen and circle.

1
(b) c a

2
c a b

B Say and circle.

1
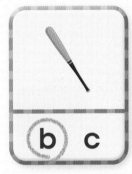
(b) c

2

c a

3

c b

C Say and write the beginning letters.

1

B b

2

Oh! My Phonics ❶

Listen and chant.

		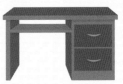
dad	**dog**	**desk**

egg	**elbow**	**elephant**

fan	**fish**	**fork**

Say and trace.

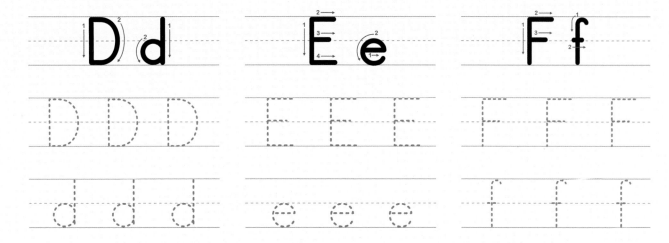

 Listen and circle.

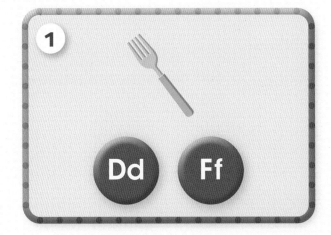

1
Dd   Ff

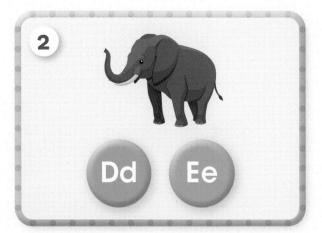

2
Dd   Ee

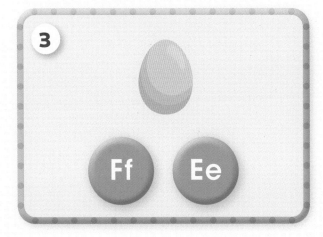

3
Ff   Ee

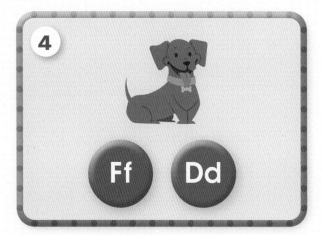

4
Ff   Dd

Circle and write. Then say.

1

Dd | Ee

2

Ee | Ff

3

Dd | Ff

 Find and color.

1 **Dd**

2 **Ee**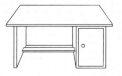

3 **Ff**

Listen and circle.

1   D   e   F   **2**   d   e   F

3   d   E   F   **4**   D   e   f

5   D   E   f   **6**   d   E   F

 Listen, match, and write.

1 og   f   d   **2** an

3 gg   e   f   **4** ish

Match and read.

1  e   ·   ·  ·   ·   fish

2 f   ·   ·  ·   ·   desk

3 d   ·   ·  ·   ·   elephant

Circle and write.

1 I have a ☐og.   d   f

2 I have a ☐ork.   e   f

3 I have an ☐gg.   e   d

Listen to the story.

I see Dad.
I see a desk.

I see an egg.
I see a fork.

I see a fish.
I see an elephant.

I see a dog.
I see a fan.

☀ **Read and circle.**

① Dad is at the fan   desk .

② An elephant   egg is on TV.

Sight Words
a   an   I   see

QUIZ UNIT 01-02

A Listen and circle.

1   a   b   d

2   d   b   c

B Say and circle.

1

e   a

2

d   f

3

a   b

C Say and write the beginning letters.

1

_____

2

_____

Gg Hh Ii

Alphabet Sounds

Listen and chant.

15

hippo

gorilla

hat

girl

hand

iguana

igloo

green

insect

Gg

girl

green

gorilla

Hh

hat

hand

hippo

Ii

igloo

iguana

insect

Say and trace.

G g   H h   I i

G G G   H H H   I I I

g g g   h h h   i i i

 Listen, circle, and check.

1

☐ Gg
✓ Hh

2

☐ Ii
☐ Hh

3

☐ Gg
☐ Ii

Match and write. Then say.

1 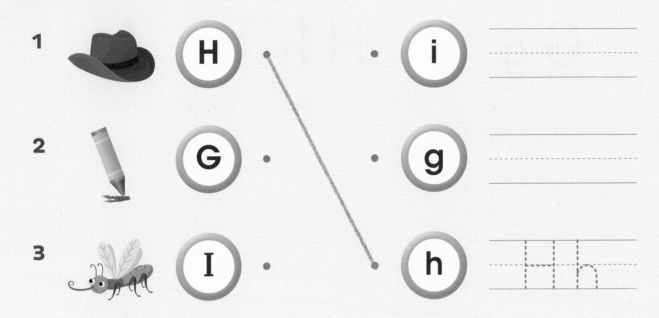 H · · i
_____

2 G · · g
_____

3 I · · h
Hh

Say and circle.

 1 Gg

 2 Ii

 3 Hh

Listen and circle.

1 G h I   **2** g H I

3 g H i   **4** G h i

5 G H i   **6** g H I

 Listen, match, and write.

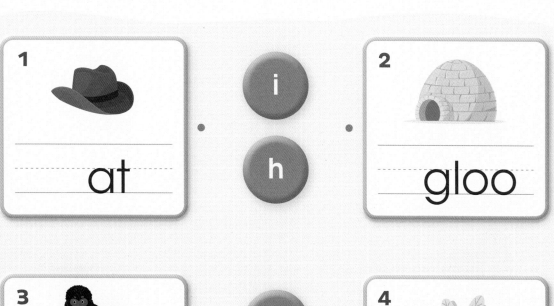

1 at

i

h

2 gloo

3 orilla

g

i

4 nsect

🎯 Match and read.

1 g · ·  · · iguana

2 i · · · · girl

3 h · · · · hand

💭 Circle and write.

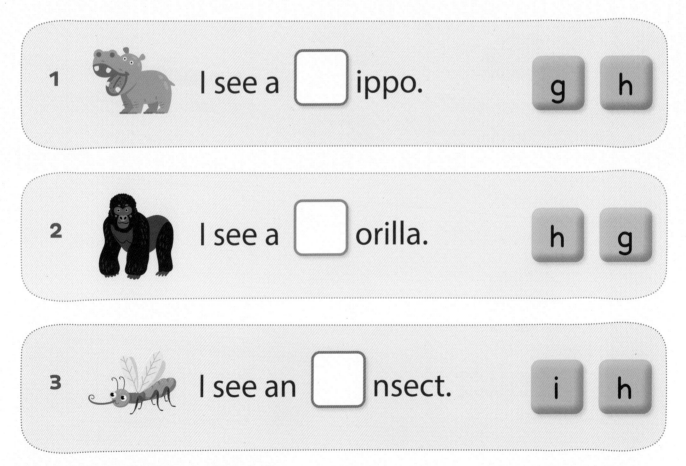

1 I see a [ ]ippo. g h

2 I see a [ ]orilla. h g

3 I see an [ ]nsect. i h

※ **Read and circle.**

1 The girl has a   hippo   hat .

2 The insect is   green   igloo .

Sight Words   are   at   look   the   they

QUIZ UNIT 02-03

A Listen and circle.

1 d e g

2 f i e

B Say and circle.

1

e f

2

g d

3

h i

C Say and write the beginning letters.

1

2

Jj Kk Ll

Listen and chant.

Jj

jam

jet

jacket

Kk

kid

kiwi

key

Ll

lamp

lemon

lion

Say and trace.

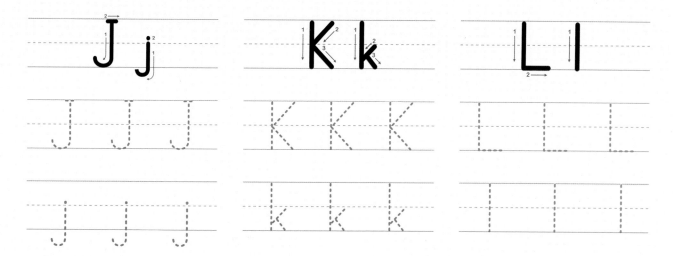

J J J

J J J

K K K

k k k

L L L

l l l

 Listen, circle, and check.

1
☐ Jj
☐ Kk

2
☐ Ll
☐ Kk

3
☐ Jj
☐ Ll

Match and write. Then say.

1 (K) • • (j) _____

2 (L) • • (k) _____

3 (J) • • (l) _____

Say and circle.

1 **Jj**

2 **Ll**

3 **Kk**

Listen and circle.

1	**J**	k	**L**	**2**	j	**K**	**L**

1   **J**   k   **L**   2   j   **K**   **L**

3   j   **K**   l   4   **J**   k   l

5   **J**   **K**   l   6   j   **K**   **L**

 Listen, match, and write.

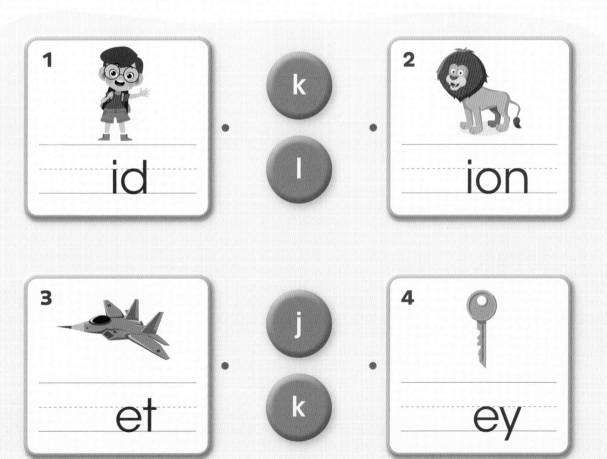

1   id

2   ion

3   et

4   ey

k   l   j   k

 **Match and read.**

1 l   • • • • lemon

2 j   • • • • jam

3 k   • • • • kiwi

 **Circle and write.**

1 This is my ☐ey.   k   l

2 This is my ☐acket.   l   j

3 This is my ☐amp.   l   k

Listen to the story.

Mom has a kiwi and a lemon. Mom makes jam.

Mom makes a jacket.

A kid makes a jet.

A kid makes a lion.

A kid makes a key.

☀ **Read and circle.**

❶ Mom makes a jet.   Yes   No

❷ A kid makes a lion.   Yes   No

Sight Words   a   and   has   makes

QUIZ UNIT 03-04

A Listen and circle.

1

j i g

2

k h l

B Say and circle.

1

l g

2

j k

3

h l

C Say and write the beginning letters.

1

_____

2

_____

REVIEW 1

Alphabet Sounds
Aa-Ll

Check the words you can read.
Then listen and repeat.

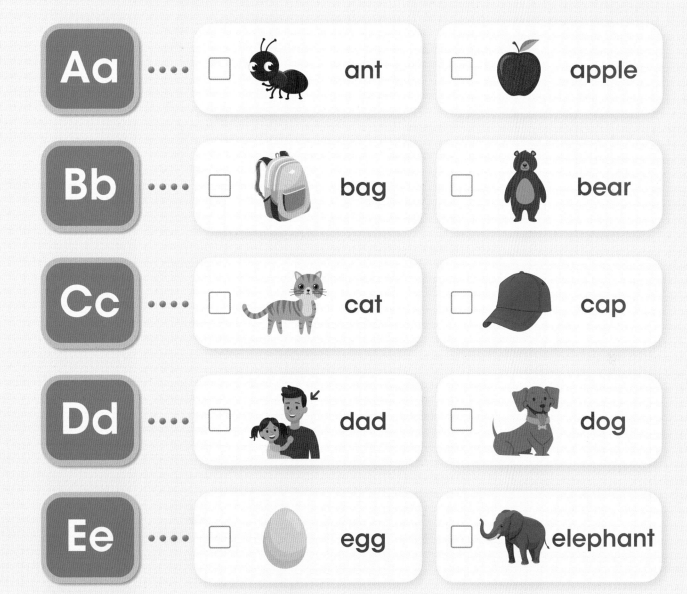

Aa ☐ ant	☐ apple
Bb ☐ bag	☐ bear
Cc ☐ cat	☐ cap
Dd ☐ dad	☐ dog
Ee ☐ egg	☐ elephant
Ff ☐ fan	☐ fish

Check the words you can read.
Then listen and repeat.

Gg ..... ☐ girl ☐ green

Hh ..... ☐ hat ☐ hand

Ii ..... ☐ igloo ☐ iguana

Jj ..... ☐ jam ☐ jet

Kk ..... ☐ kid ☐ kiwi

Ll ..... ☐ lamp ☐ lion

A Listen, write, and circle.

1

2

B Listen and match.

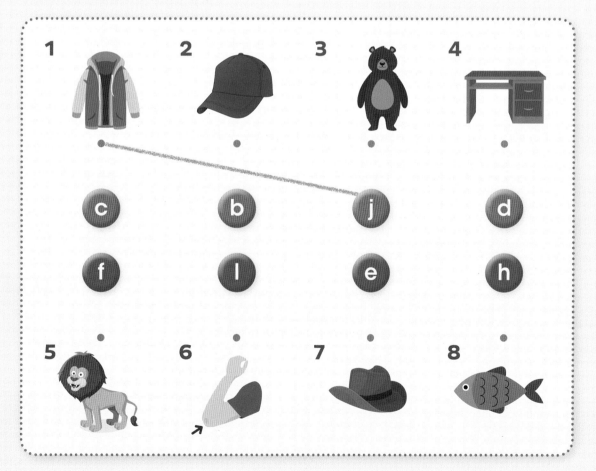

1   2   3   4

c   b   j   d

f   l   e   h

5   6   7   8

C Color the beginning sound.

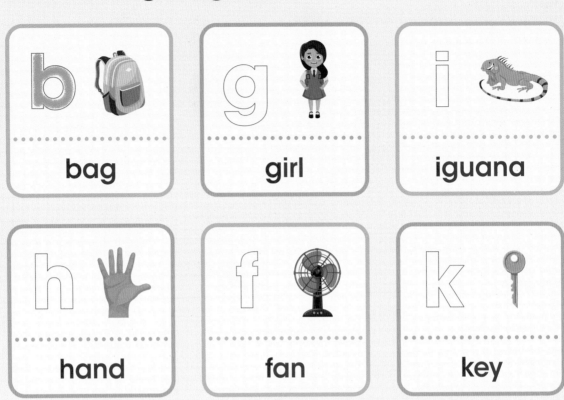

| b bag | g girl | i iguana |
| h hand | f fan | k key |

D Circle and write.

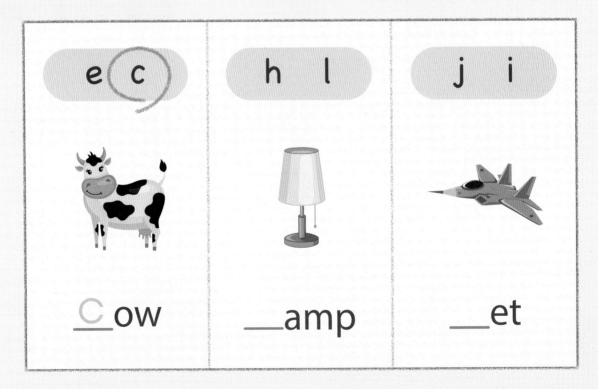

| e (c) | h l | j i |
| c ow | __ amp | __ et |

E Circle the correct picture.

F Listen and circle.

Say and write.

a   f   e   i   k   d

1

fork

2

lephant

3

ad

4

nt

5

id

6

gloo

H Circle the pictures with the same beginning sound.
Then write.

1   Bb

2

3

4

5

I **Say and circle the correct pair.**

1. i / a
2. d / h
3. k / e
4. g / f

J **Read and write.**

jacket   fish   insect

1 **F** is for 🐟 _____ .

2 **I** is for 🦟 _____ .

mask   **mat**   **monkey**

   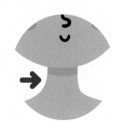

nest   **nose**   **neck**

ox   **octopus**   **ostrich**

Say and trace.

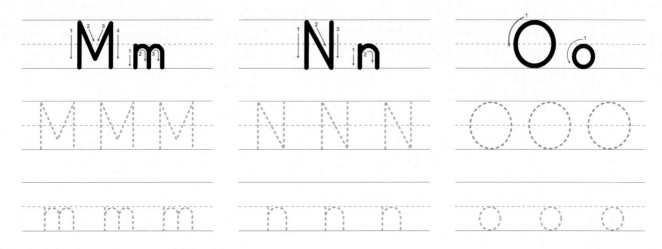

 Listen and circle.

1 Mm Oo

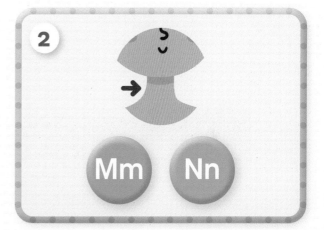

2 Mm Nn

3 Mm Nn

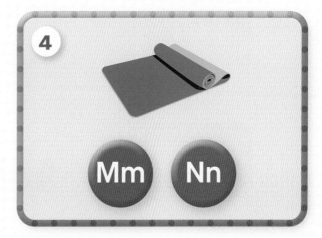

4 Mm Nn

Circle and write. Then say.

1

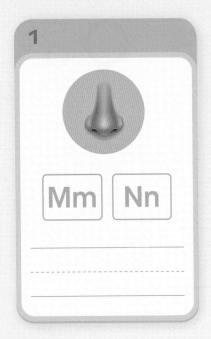

Mm	Nn

_____

2

Nn	Oo

_____

3

Mm	Oo

_____

 Find and color.

1 **Mm**

2 **Nn**

3 **Oo**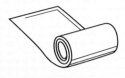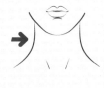

Listen and circle.

1 M n O   2 m n O

3 M N O   4 m N O

5 m N O   6 M n o

 Listen, match, and write.

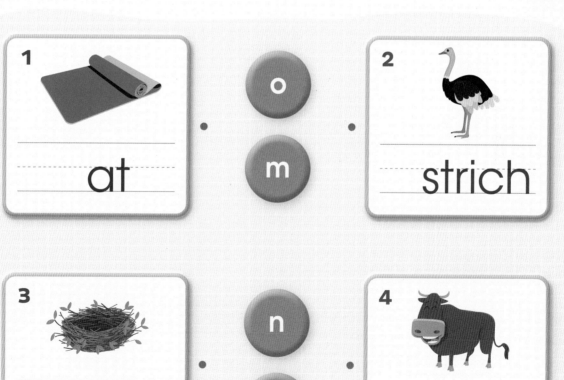

1
___at

o

m

2
___strich

3
___est

n

o

4
___x

🎯 Match and read.

1 **m** ·   · · **octopus**

2 **n** ·   · · **neck**

3 **o** ·   · · **monkey**

💭 Circle and write.

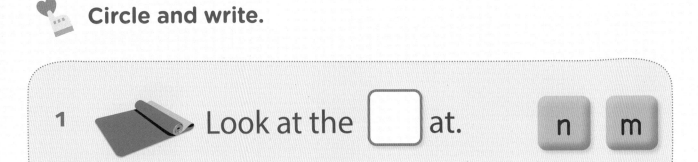

1 Look at the ☐ at.   **n** **m**

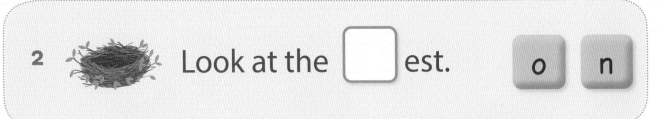

2 Look at the ☐ est.   **o** **n**

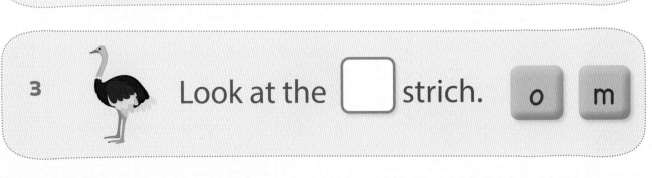

3 Look at the ☐ strich.   **o** **m**

☀ **Read and circle.**

1 The kids wear masks.　　Yes　No

2 There is one ox mask.　　Yes　No

Sight Words　　a　an　I　see　we　your

QUIZ UNIT 04-05

A Listen and circle.

1   j   k   m

2   m   l   k

B Say and circle.

1   n   m

2   j   k

3   m   l

C Say and write the beginning letters.

1
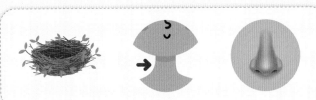
_____

2

_____

• **Listen and chant.**

pig

pink

panda

queen

quiet

question

red

rug

rose

Say and trace.

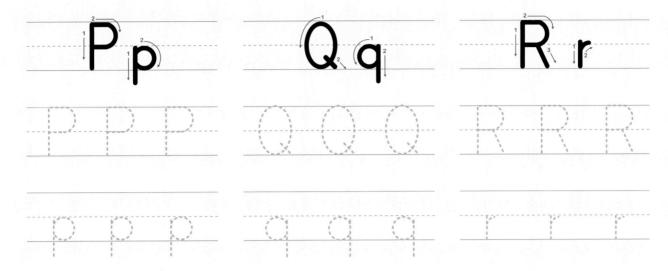

 Listen and circle.

1
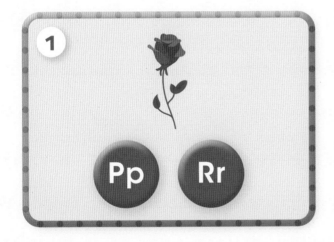

2
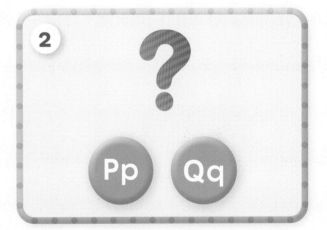

3
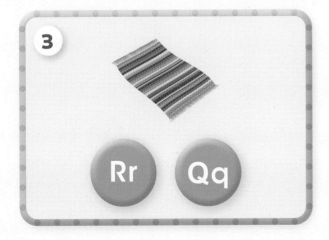

4

Circle and write. Then say.

1

| Pp | Qq |

_____

- - - - - - - - - - - -

_____

2

| Qq | Rr |

_____

- - - - - - - - - - - -

_____

3

| Pp | Rr |

_____

- - - - - - - - - - - -

_____

 Find and color.

1 Pp

2 Qq

3 Rr

Listen and circle.

1. P q R
2. p q R
3. P Q r
4. p Q R
5. p Q r
6. P q r

 Listen, match, and write.

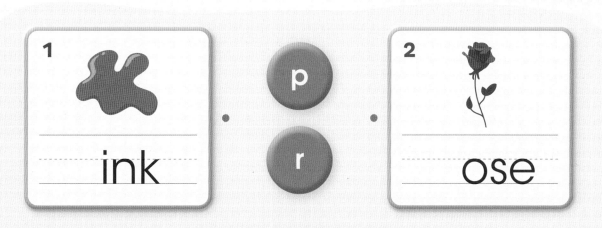

1. ink
2. ose

p

r

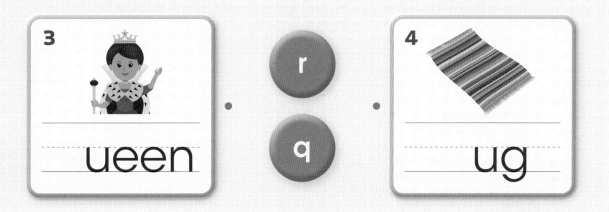

3. ueen
4. ug

r

q

🎯 **Match and read.**

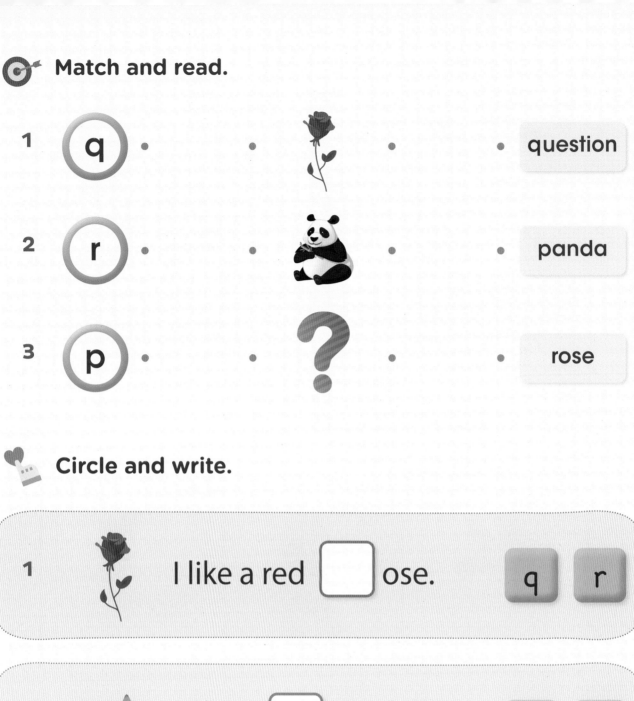

1 q · · 🌹 · · question

2 r · · 🐼 · · panda

3 p · · ❓ · · rose

🎩 **Circle and write.**

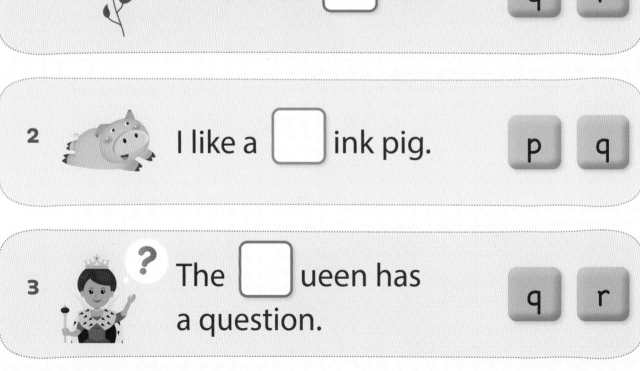

1 🌹 I like a red ☐ ose.   **q** **r**

2 🐷 I like a ☐ ink pig.   **p** **q**

3 👑❓ The ☐ ueen has a question.   **q** **r**

Listen to the story.

☀️ **Read and circle.**

① The pig has a [pink] [red] rose.

② The [queen] [panda] has a rug.

Sight Words	a be for is it please what

QUIZ UNIT 05-06

A Listen and circle.

1 p q n

2 m o r

B Say and circle.

1

p m

2

o r

3

n q

C Say and write the beginning letters.

1

2

Ss

six

sock

Tt

ten

top

Uu

under

umbrella

Vv

vase

vest

Say and trace.

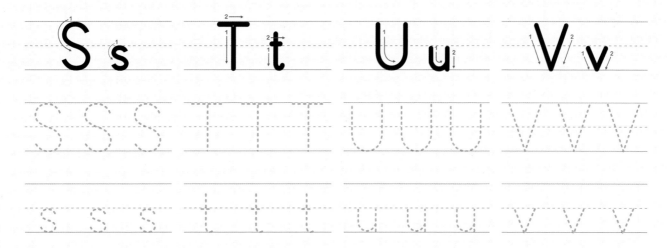

 Listen, circle, and check.

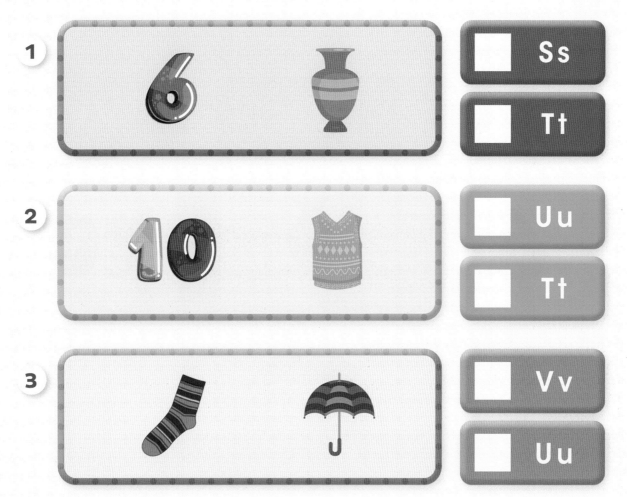

1

	Ss
	Tt

2

	Uu
	Tt

3

	Vv
	Uu

Match and write. Then say.

1   (T) ·   · (u) _____

2   (U) ·   · (s) _____

3   (S) ·   · (t) _____

Say and circle.

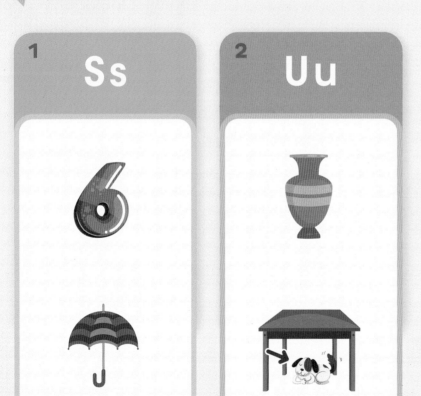

| 1 Ss | 2 Uu | 3 Vv |

Listen and circle.

1 S u V

2 s U T

3 T u s

4 V u S

5 V U t

6 s t V

 Listen, match, and write.

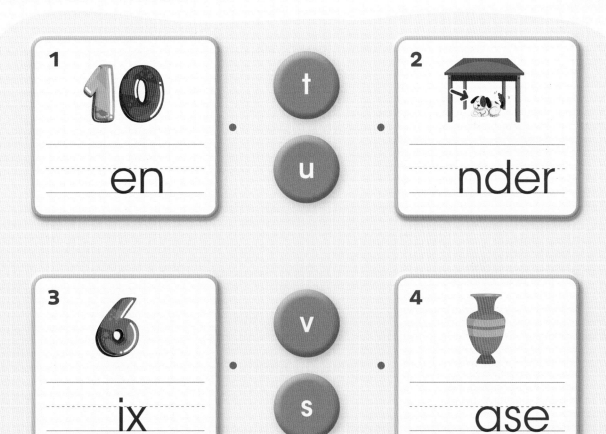

1 10 ___ en   · t ·   2 ___ nder

                   u

3 6 ___ ix   · v ·   4 ___ ase

                   s

 **Match and read.**

1 (u) • •  • • umbrella

2 (v) • • • • top

3 (t) • • • • vest

 Circle and write.

1 A bear ☐nder the tree.   **t** **u**

2 ☐ix eggs in the nest.   **S** **U**

3 A rose in the ☐ase.   **v** **s**

Listen to the story.

It's Christmas!

A sock.
A sock on the tree.

Six gifts.
Six gifts under the tree.

And snow!
Merry Christmas!

Ten roses.
Ten roses in the vase.

Read and circle.

1. A [sock] [vest] on the tree.

2. [Ten] [Six] gifts under the tree.

Sight Words   a   and   in   it's   on   the

QUIZ UNIT 06-07

A Listen and circle.

1

p u t

2

s v q

B Say and circle.

1

s u

2

t r

3

p v

C Say and write the beginning letters.

1

_____

_____

2

_____

_____

• Listen and chant.

Ww	 wolf	 water
Xx	 box	 fox
Yy	 yo-yo	yellow
Zz	 zoo	 zebra

Say and trace.

W w   X x   Y y   Z z

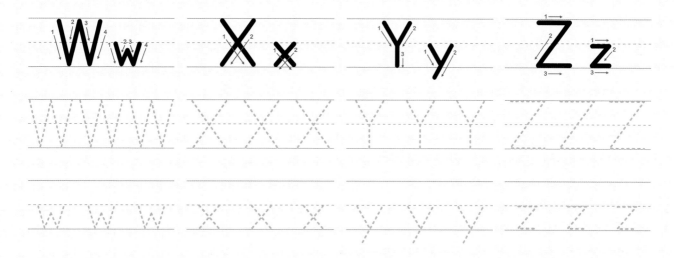

 Listen, circle, and check.

57

1

Ww

Xx

2

Xx

Zz

3

Vv

Yy

Match and write. Then say.

1 (W) •   • (y) _____

2 (Z) •   • (z) _____

3  (Y) •   • (w) _____

 Say and circle.

1 Yy

2 Xx

3 Zz

Listen and circle.

1   **W**   y   Z

2   X   y   W

3   Z   w   x

4   w   Z   Y

5   w   Y   X

6   x   Y   w

 Listen, match, and write.

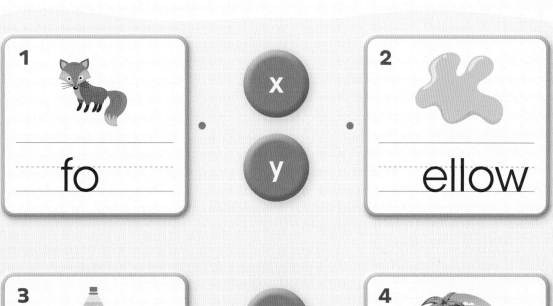

1   fo____

2   ____ellow

3   ____ater

4   ____oo

x   y   z   w

 **Match and read.**

1   x   •   •   🟫   •   •   yo-yo

2   y   •   •   🦓   •   •   box

3   z   •   •   🪀   •   •   zebra

 **Circle and write.**

1   They are [ ] ellow.   w   y

2   A [ ] olf is in the zoo.   x   w

3   A cap is in the bo [ ] .   z   x

Listen to the story.

☀ **Read and circle.**

1 They see a fox and a bear.   Yes   No

2 The animals drink water.   Yes   No

Sight Words   a   are   at   is   that   the   they   we

QUIZ UNIT 07-08

A Listen and circle.

1   y   v   t

2   x   u   w

B Say and circle.

1

s   y

2

x   z

3

w   s

C Say and write the beginning letters.

1

2

**Check the words you can read.
Then listen and repeat.**

Mm ·····

☐ mask   ☐ monkey

Nn ·····

☐ nest   ☐ nose

Oo ·····

☐ ox   ☐ octopus

Pp ·····

☐ pig   ☐ panda

Qq ·····

☐ queen   ☐ quiet

Rr ·····

☐ red   ☐ rug

Ss ·····

☐ six   ☐ sock

Check the words you can read.
Then listen and repeat.

Tt ..... ☐ 10 ten ☐ top

Uu ..... ☐ under ☐ umbrella

Vv ..... ☐ vase ☐ vest

Ww ..... ☐ wolf ☐ water

Xx ..... ☐ box ☐ fox

Yy ..... ☐ yo-yo ☐ yellow

Zz ..... ☐ zoo ☐ zebra

A Listen, write, and circle.

1

2

B Listen and match.

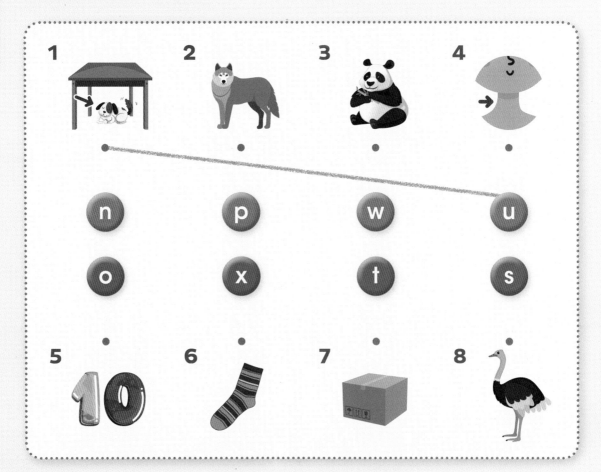

C Color the beginning sound.

| q queen | m mat | u umbrella |
| ox | t top | v vest |

D Circle and write.

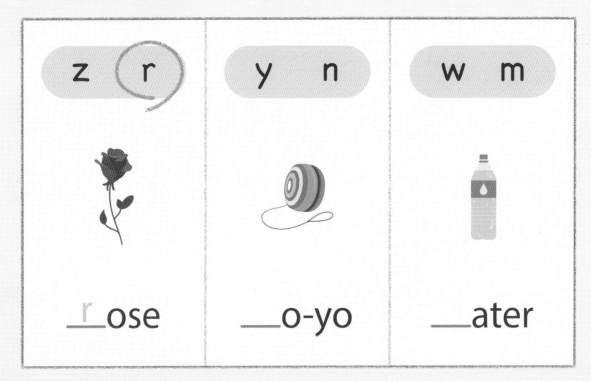

| z (r) | y n | w m |
| __rose | __o-yo | __ater |

E Circle the correct picture.

F Listen and circle.

G **Say and write.**

| n | q | p̶ | y | x | v |

1

pig

2

___ose

3

___ellow

4

___ase

5

fo___

6

___uestion

H **Circle the pictures with the same beginning sound. Then write.**

I Say and circle the correct pair.

1 n v

2 t u

3 p y

4 s q

J Read and write.

yellow   octopus   pink

1 **O** is for  _____ .

2 **Y** is for _____ .

WORD LIST

• **Can you read? Read and check.**

UNIT 01

1. ☐ ant
2. ☐ apple
3. ☐ alligator
4. ☐ bag
5. ☐ bat
6. ☐ bear
7. ☐ cat
8. ☐ cap
9. ☐ cow

UNIT 02

10. ☐ dad
11. ☐ dog
12. ☐ desk
13. ☐ egg
14. ☐ elbow
15. ☐ elephant
16. ☐ fan
17. ☐ fish
18. ☐ fork

UNIT 03

19	☐	girl
20	☐	green
21	☐	gorilla
22	☐	hat
23	☐	hand
24	☐	hippo
25	☐	igloo
26	☐	iguana
27	☐	insect

UNIT 04

28	☐	jam
29	☐	jet
30	☐	jacket
31	☐	kid
32	☐	kiwi
33	☐	key
34	☐	lamp
35	☐	lemon
36	☐	lion

WORD LIST

• **Can you read? Read and check.**

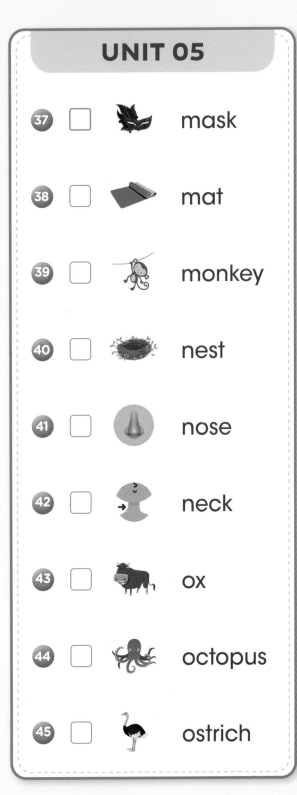

UNIT 05

- 37 ☐ mask
- 38 ☐ mat
- 39 ☐ monkey
- 40 ☐ nest
- 41 ☐ nose
- 42 ☐ neck
- 43 ☐ ox
- 44 ☐ octopus
- 45 ☐ ostrich

UNIT 06

- 46 ☐ pig
- 47 ☐ pink
- 48 ☐ panda
- 49 ☐ queen
- 50 ☐ quiet
- 51 ☐ question
- 52 ☐ red
- 53 ☐ rug
- 54 ☐ rose

UNIT 07

55	☐	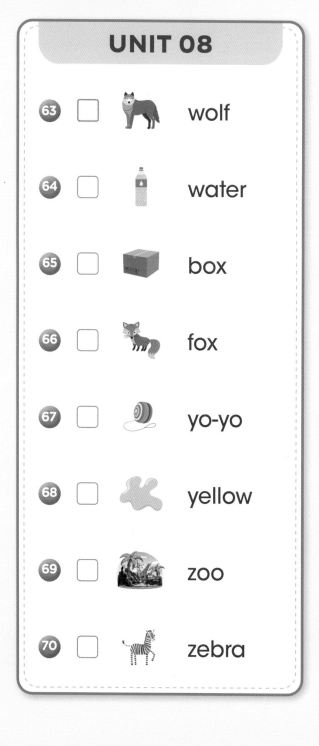 six
56	☐	sock
57	☐	ten
58	☐	top
59	☐	under
60	☐	umbrella
61	☐	vase
62	☐	vest

UNIT 08

63	☐	wolf
64	☐	water
65	☐	box
66	☐	fox
67	☐	yo-yo
68	☐	yellow
69	☐	zoo
70	☐	zebra

SIGHT WORD LIST

• **Can you read? Read and check.**

1. ☐ a — 13, 21, 37, 53, 61, 69, 77
2. ☐ an — 13, 21, 53
3. ☐ and — 37, 69
4. ☐ are — 29, 77
5. ☐ at — 29, 77
6. ☐ be — 61
7. ☐ for — 61
8. ☐ has — 37
9. ☐ I — 21, 53
10. ☐ in — 69
11. ☐ is — 13, 61, 77
12. ☐ it — 61
13. ☐ it's — 69
14. ☐ look — 29
15. ☐ makes — 37

16. ☐ on — 69
17. ☐ please — 61
18. ☐ see — 21, 53
19. ☐ that — 77
20. ☐ the — 29, 69, 77
21. ☐ they — 29, 77
22. ☐ this — 13
23. ☐ we — 53, 77
24. ☐ what — 61
25. ☐ your — 53

SCOPE & SEQUENCE

Book 1 — Alphabet Sounds

UNIT 01	Aa Bb Cc
UNIT 02	Dd Ee Ff
UNIT 03	Gg Hh Ii
UNIT 04	Jj Kk Ll
UNIT 05	Mm Nn Oo
UNIT 06	Pp Qq Rr
UNIT 07	Ss Tt Uu Vv
UNIT 08	Ww Xx Yy Zz

Book 2 — Short Vowels

UNIT 01	Short Vowel a: am, ag, ap
UNIT 02	Short Vowel a: ad, an, at
UNIT 03	Short Vowel i: ig, in, ip
UNIT 04	Short Vowel i: id, it, ix
UNIT 05	Short Vowel e: ed, en, et
UNIT 06	Short Vowel o: og, ot, ox
UNIT 07	Short Vowel u: ug, un, up
UNIT 08	Short Vowel u: ub, ud, ut

Book 3 — Long Vowels

UNIT 01	Short Vowels Review
UNIT 02	Long Vowel a: a_e
UNIT 03	Long Vowel a: a_e
UNIT 04	Long Vowel i: i_e
UNIT 05	Long Vowel i: i_e
UNIT 06	Long Vowel o: o_e
UNIT 07	Long Vowel o: o_e
UNIT 08	Long Vowel u: u_e

Book 4 — Double Letters

UNIT 01	Consonant Blends : bl, fl, gl, sl
UNIT 02	Consonant Blends : br, cr, dr, gr
UNIT 03	Consonant Blends : sm, sn, st, sw
UNIT 04	Consonant Digraphs : sh, ch, th, ng
UNIT 05	Vowel Digraphs : ai, ay Vowel Diphthongs : oi, oy
UNIT 06	Vowel Digraphs : oa, ow1 (snow) Vowel Diphthongs : ou, ow2 (cow)
UNIT 07	R-controlled Vowels : ar, or, ir, er
UNIT 08	Vowel Digraphs: ee, ea, short oo, long oo

MEMO

MEMO

UNIT 01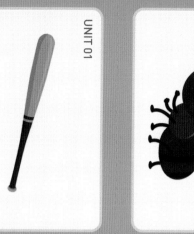

UNIT 01

UNIT 01

UNIT 02

UNIT 01

UNIT 02

UNIT 02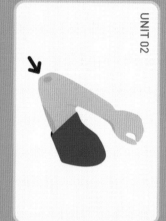

UNIT 01

UNIT 01

UNIT 02

UNIT 02

UNIT 01

UNIT 01

UNIT 02

UNIT 02

ant

apple

alligator

bag

bat

bear

cat

cap

cow

dad

dog

desk

egg

elbow

elephant

fan

UNIT 04
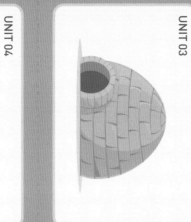

UNIT 03

UNIT 03

UNIT 02

UNIT 04

UNIT 03

UNIT 03

UNIT 02

UNIT 04

UNIT 03

UNIT 03

UNIT 03

UNIT 04

UNIT 04

UNIT 03

UNIT 03

fish

fork

girl

green

gorilla

hat

hand

hippo

igloo

iguana

insect

jam

jet

jacket

kid

kiwi

UNIT 05 UNIT 05 UNIT 05 UNIT 04

UNIT 06 UNIT 05 UNIT 05 UNIT 04

UNIT 06 UNIT 05 UNIT 05 UNIT 04

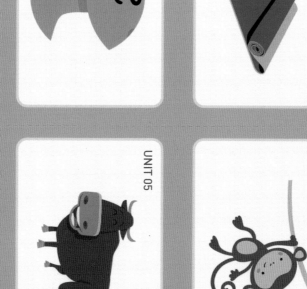

UNIT 06 UNIT 05 UNIT 05 UNIT 04

key

mask

nose

ostrich

lamp

mat

neck

pig

lemon

monkey

ox

pink

lion

nest

octopus

panda

UNIT 07

UNIT 07

UNIT 06

UNIT 06

UNIT 07

UNIT 07

UNIT 06

UNIT 06

UNIT 08

UNIT 07

UNIT 07

UNIT 06

UNIT 08

UNIT 07

UNIT 07

UNIT 06

queen

rug

ten

vase

quiet

rose

top

vest

question

six

under

wolf

red

sock

umbrella

water

UNIT 08

UNIT 08

UNIT 08

UNIT 08

UNIT 08

UNIT 08

box

zoo

fox

zebra

yo-yo

yellow

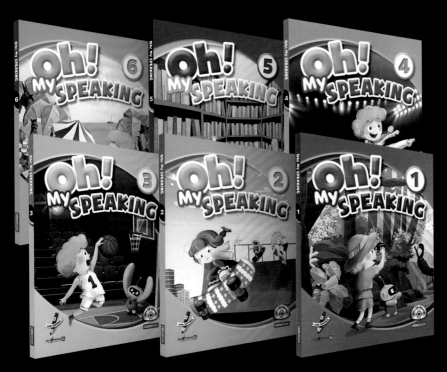

Oh! My SPEAKING

오! 마이 스피킹

대상	예비 초 ~ 초등 4학년
구성	**Student Book**
	Workbook, MP3 CD, Picture Cards 포함

① 레벨 1 ~ 6으로 세분화된 레벨링

② 의사소통 중심의 수업을 위해
교사와 학생 모두에게 최적화된 구성

③ 전략적 반복 학습의 나선형 시스템

④ 말하기를 중심으로
어휘, 문법까지 통합적 학습 가능

오! 마이 스피킹 교재 특징

수준별 학습을 위한
6권 분류

1권 / 2권	Early Beginners
3권 / 4권	Beginners
5권 / 6권	Pre-Intermediates

세이펜 적용 도서

세이펜으로
원어민 발음을
학습하고, 혼자서도
재미있게 학습해요!

SAYPEN

워크북 숙제도우미,
Christina(초코언니)

워크북 속 QR코드와
세이펜으로
Christina의 음성을
들을 수 있어요!

① 구문

판매 1위 '천일문' 콘텐츠를 활용하여 정확하고 다양한 구문 학습

(끊어읽기) (해석하기) (문장 구조 분석) (해설·해석 제공) (단어 스크램블링) (영작하기)

② 문법·서술형

쎄듀의 모든 문법 문항을 활용하여 내신까지 해결하는 정교한 문법 유형 제공

(객관식과 주관식의 결합) (문법 포인트별 학습) (보기를 활용한 집합 문항) (내신대비 서술형) (어법+서술형 문제)

③ 어휘

초·중·고·공무원까지 방대한 어휘량을 제공하며 오프라인 TEST 인쇄도 가능

(영단어 카드 학습) (단어 ↔ 뜻 유형) (예문 활용 유형) (단어 매칭 게임)

④ 선생님 보유 문항 이용

(Online Test) (OMR Test)

with 세이펜

원어민 발음을 실시간 반복학습	단어 및 문장의 우리말 해석 듣기	발음을 듣고 따라 해보며 혼자서도 쉽게 학습

세이펜 핀파일 다운로드 안내

STEP ① 세이펜과 컴퓨터를 USB 케이블로 연결하세요.

STEP ② 쎄듀북 홈페이지(www.cedubook.com)에 접속 후, 학습자료실 메뉴에서 학습할 교재를 찾아 이동합니다.

> 초등교재 ▶ ELT ▶ 학습교재 클릭 ▶ 세이펜 핀파일 자료 클릭
> ▶ 다운로드 (저장을 '다른 이름으로 저장'으로 변경하여 저장소를 USB로 변경) ▶ 완료

STEP ③ 음원 다운로드가 완료되면 세이펜과 컴퓨터의 USB 케이블을 분리하세요.

STEP ④ 세이펜을 분리하면 "시스템을 초기화 중입니다. 잠시만 기다려 주세요."라는 멘트가 나옵니다.

STEP ⑤ 멘트 종료 후 세이펜을 〈Oh! My Phonics〉 표지에 대보세요.
효과음이 나온 후 바로 학습을 시작할 수 있습니다.

참고사항

◆ 세이펜은 본 교재에 포함되어 있지 않습니다. 별도로 구매하여 이용할 수 있으며, 기존에 보유하신 세이펜이 있다면 핀파일만 다운로드해서
  바로 이용하실 수 있습니다.

◆ 세이펜에서 제작된 모든 기종(기존에 보유하고 계신 기종도 호환 가능)으로 사용이 가능합니다.

◆ 모든 기종은 세이펜에서 권장하는 최신 펌웨어 업데이트를 진행해 주시기 바랍니다.
  업데이트는 세이펜 홈페이지(www.saypen.com)에서 가능합니다.

◆ 핀파일은 쎄듀북 홈페이지(www.cedubook.com)와 세이펜 홈페이지(www.saypen.com)에서 모두 다운로드 가능합니다.

◆ 세이펜을 이용하지 않는 학습자는 쎄듀북 홈페이지 부가학습자료, 교재 내 QR코드 이미지 등을 활용하여 원어민 음성으로 학습하실 수 있습니다.

◆ 기타 문의사항은 www.cedubook.com / 02-3272-4766으로 연락 바랍니다.

Oh! My Phonics

Oh! My

Phonics

Alphabet Sounds

1

Workbook

Oh! My Phonics

Alphabet Sounds

1

Workbook

CONTENTS

A Trace and write.

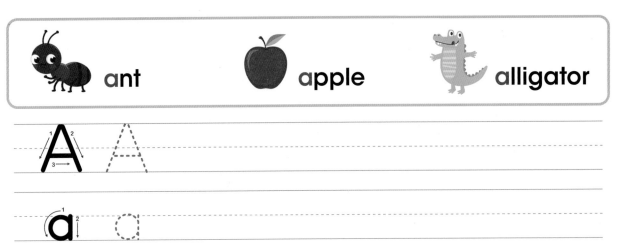

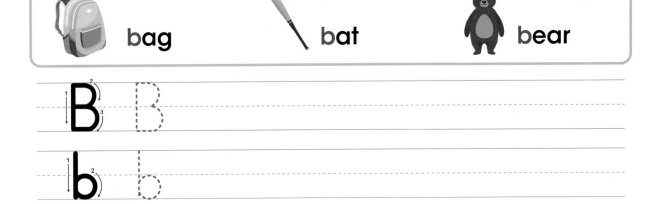

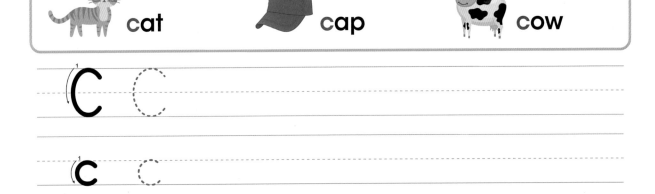

B Circle and write.

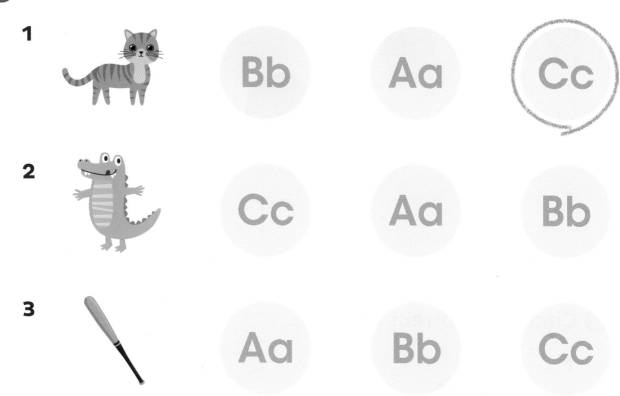

1   Bb   Aa   (Cc)

2   Cc   Aa   Bb

3   Aa   Bb   Cc

C Look and circle.

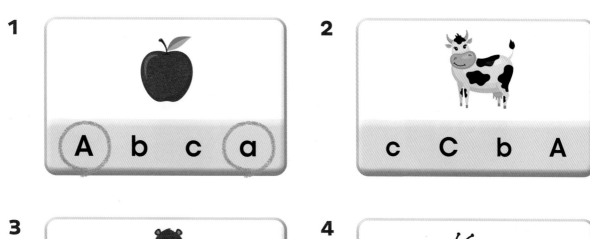

1   (A)   b   c   (a)

2   c   C   b   A

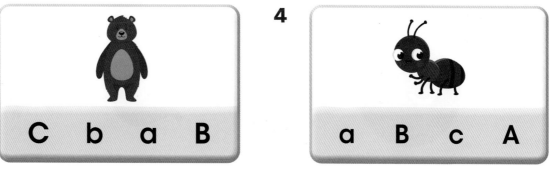

3   C   b   a   B

4   a   B   c   A

D Write the beginning letter.

1

ant

2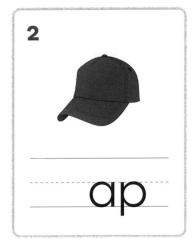

ap

3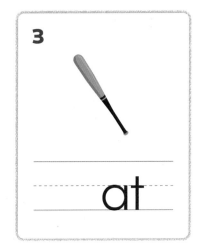

at

E Circle the correct pictures.

1

2

3

A Trace and write.

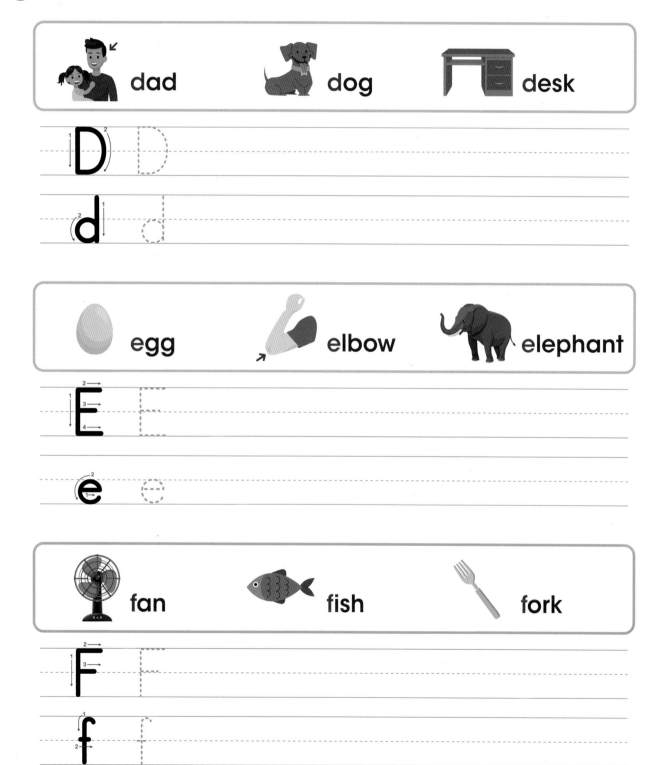

B Circle and write.

1  Ee Dd Ff

2   Ff Dd Ee

3   Dd Ee Ff

C Look and circle.

1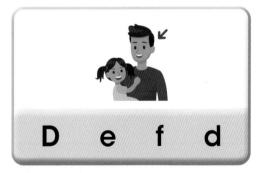
D e f d

2
E f d F

3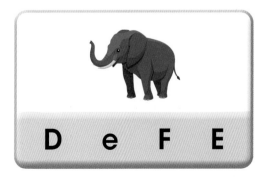
D e F E

4
d E F f

D Write the beginning letter.

1

esk

2

ish

3
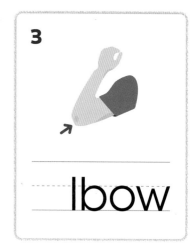
lbow

E Circle the correct pictures.

1

2
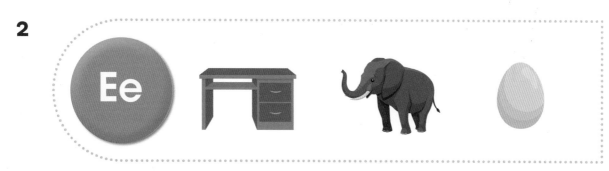

3
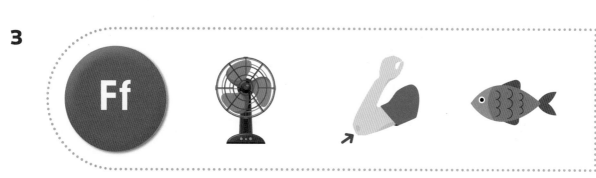

A Trace and write.

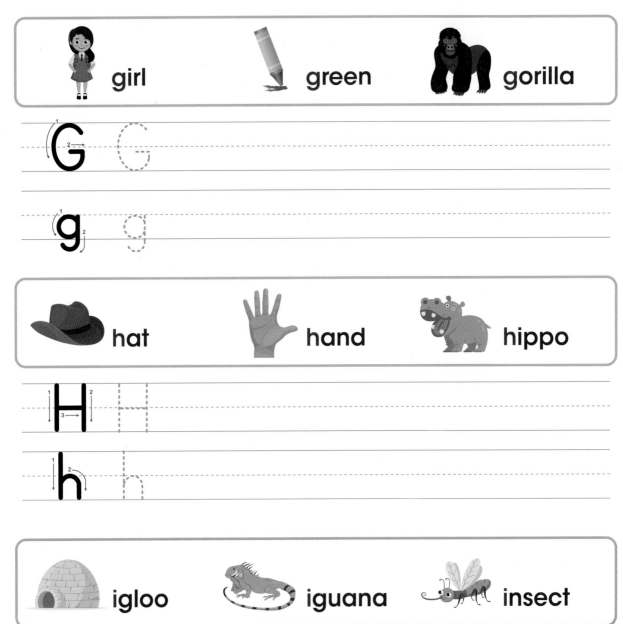

girl   green   gorilla

G G G

g g g

hat   hand   hippo

H H

h h

igloo   iguana   insect

I I

i i

B Circle and write.

1    Hh   Gg   Ii

2   Ii   Gg   Hh

3    Gg   Ii   Hh

C Look and circle.

1

G   i   g   h

2

H   h   G   I

3

I   g   h   G

4

i   H   I   g

D Write the beginning letter.

1 ____reen

2 ____and

3 ____gloo

E Circle the correct pictures.

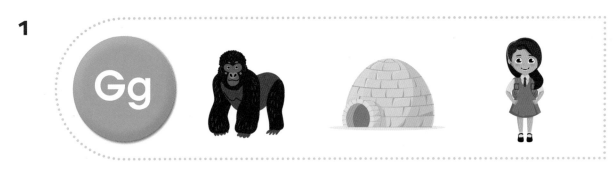

1

2

3

A Trace and write.

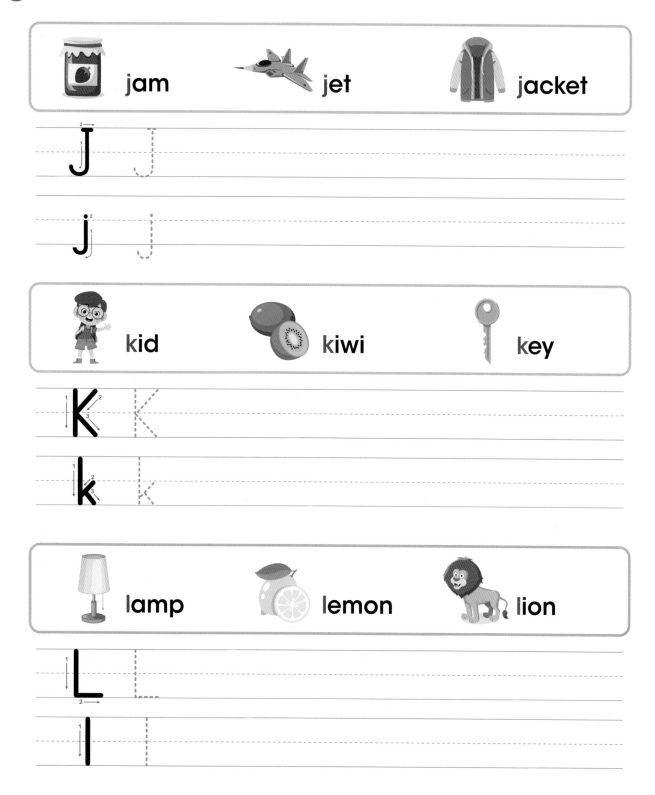

jam   jet   jacket

J   J

j   j

kid   kiwi   key

K   K

k   k

lamp   lemon   lion

L   L

l   l

B Circle and write.

1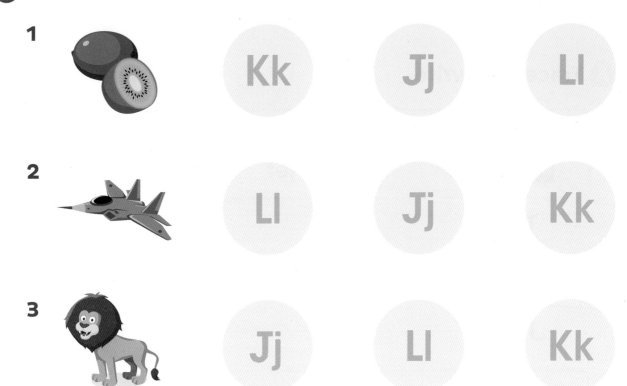

Kk   Jj   Ll

2

Ll   Jj   Kk

3

Jj   Ll   Kk

C Look and circle.

1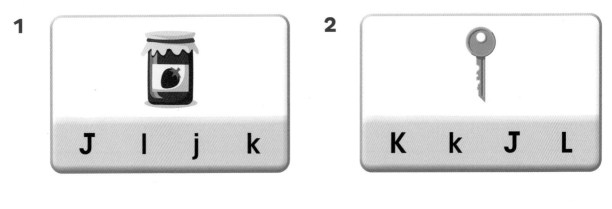

J   l   j   k

2

K   k   J   L

3

J   L   l   K

4

K   J   L   j

D Write the beginning letter.

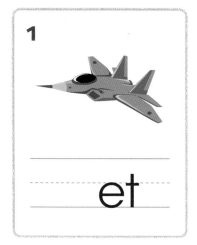
1 ___et

2 ___id

3 ___emon

E Circle the correct pictures.

1

2

3

A Look and match.

1 Bb
2 Ll
3 Gg
4 Jj
5 Ee

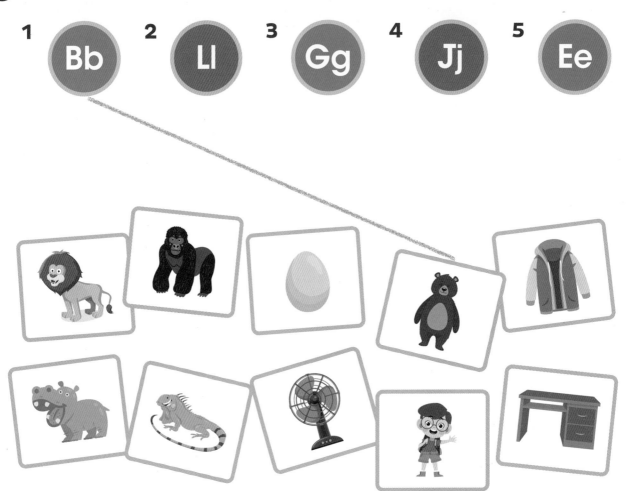

6 Ff
7 Dd
8 Kk
9 Ii
10 Hh

B Write the beginning letters.

1

HhHh

2

3

4

5

6

7

8

9

10

11

12

C Circle the correct beginning letters.

1

(L) I h

2

b g d

3

D E J

4

b E K

5

G c A

6

e H f

D Circle the pictures with the same beginning sound.

1

Kk

2

Aa

A Trace and write.

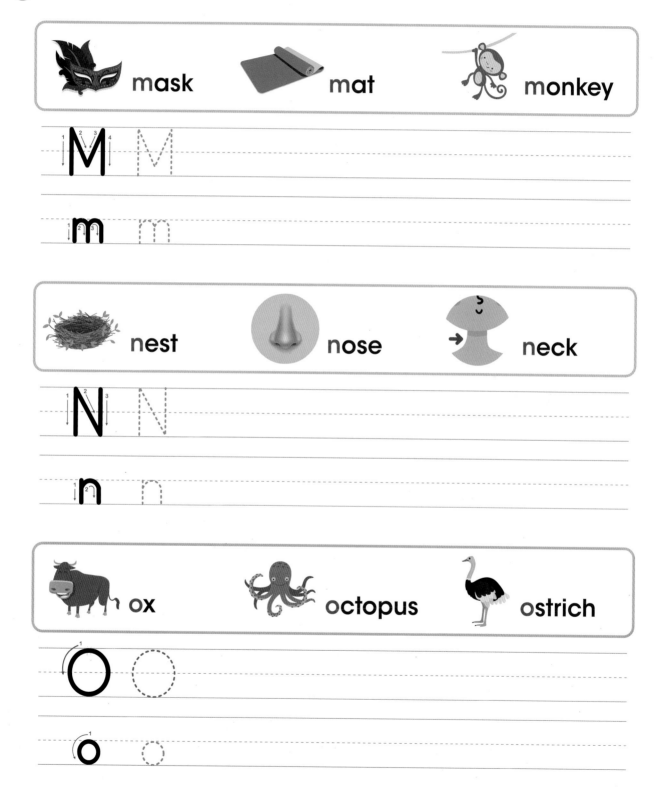

mask   mat   monkey

M   M   M

m   m

nest   nose   neck

N   N   N

n   n

ox   octopus   ostrich

O   O

o   o

B Circle and write.

1  Nn   Mm   Oo

2  Mm   Oo   Nn

3  Oo   Mm   Nn

C Look and circle.

1

M   n   N   o

2

o   N   O   M

3

M   O   n   N

4

m   N   O   M

D Write the beginning letter.

1

x

2
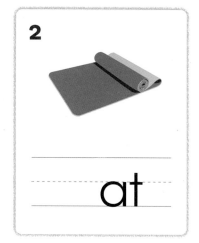
at

3
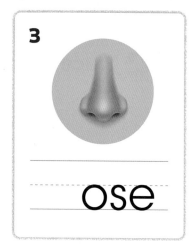
ose

E Circle the correct pictures.

1

2

3
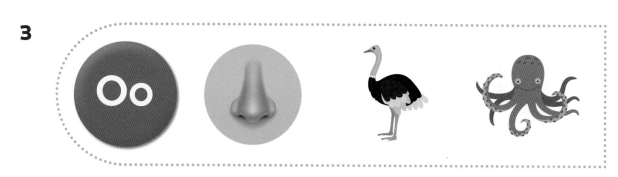

A Trace and write.

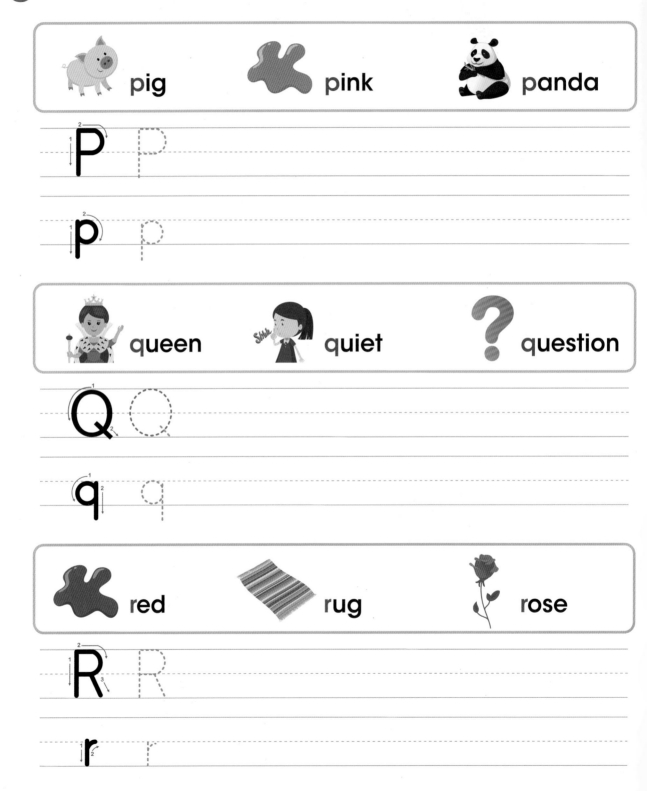

pig   pink   panda

P   P

p   p

queen   quiet   question

Q   O

q   q

red   rug   rose

R   R

r   r

B Circle and write.

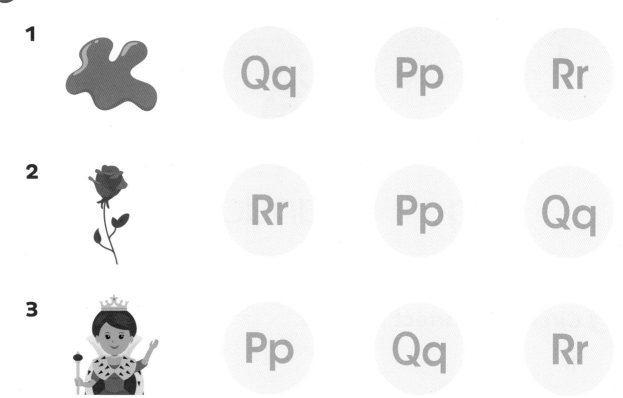

1.   Qq   Pp   Rr

2.   Rr   Pp   Qq

3.   Pp   Qq   Rr

C Look and circle.

1. ?   P   q   r   Q

2.   r   Q   R   P

3.   R   P   q   Q

4.   p   Q   R   P

D Write the beginning letter.

1
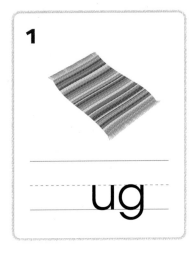

___

ug

2

___

anda

3

___

ueen

E Circle the correct pictures.

1

2

3

A Trace and write.

 six   sock

 ten   top

 under   umbrella

 vase   vest

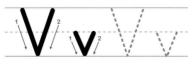

B Circle and write.

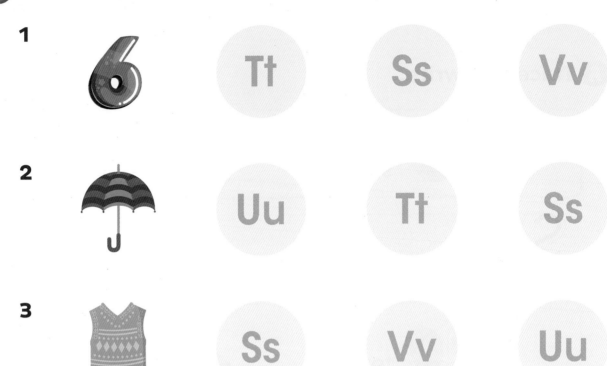

1. Tt   Ss   Vv

2. Uu   Tt   Ss

3. Ss   Vv   Uu

C Look and circle.

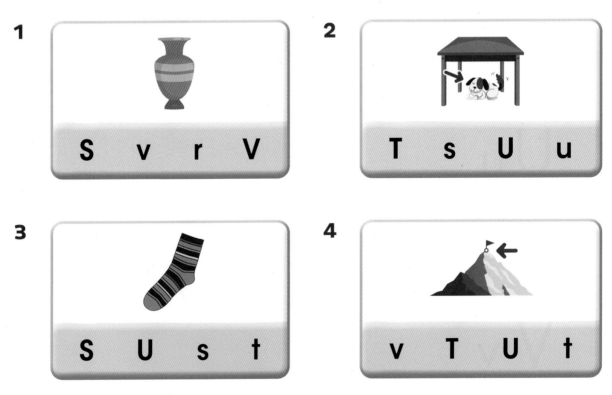

1. S   v   r   V

2. T   s   U   u

3. S   U   s   t

4. v   T   U   t

D Write the beginning letter.

1

_____
en

2

_____
nder

3

_____
ix

E Circle the correct pictures.

1

Vv

2

Tt

3

Uu

A Trace and write.

 wolf   water

W w

 box   fox

X x

 yo-yo   yellow

Y y

 zoo   zebra

Z z

B Circle and write.

1    Xx   Ww   Zz

2    Yy   Xx   Ww

3    Zz   Ww   Yy

C Look and circle.

1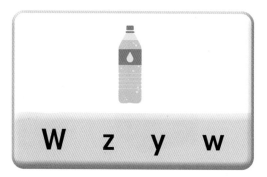

W   z   y   w

2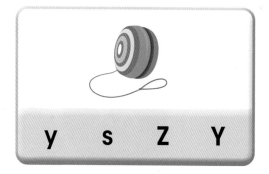

y   s   Z   Y

3

x   Y   X   w

4

W   z   Y   Z

D Write the beginning or ending letter.

1

bo___

2

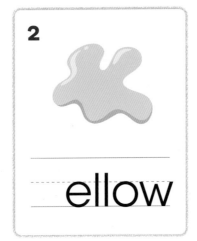

___ellow

3

___oo

E Circle the correct pictures.

1

2

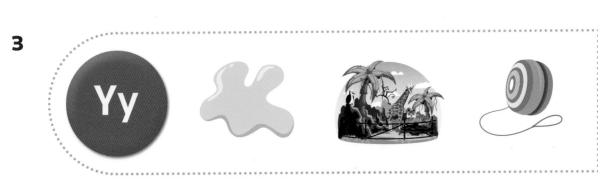

3

A Look and match.

1 Uu 2 Ww 3 Pp 4 Oo 5 Zz

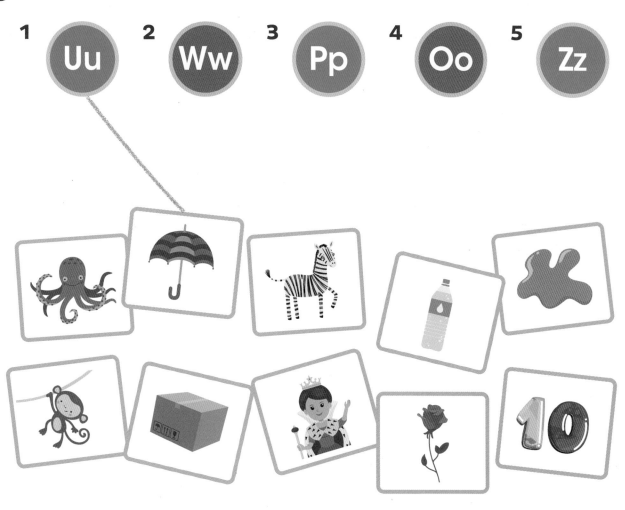

6 Qq 7 Xx 8 Rr 9 Mm 10 Tt

B Write the beginning or ending letters.

1

YyYy

2

3

4

5

6

7

8

9

10

11

12

C Circle the correct beginning letters.

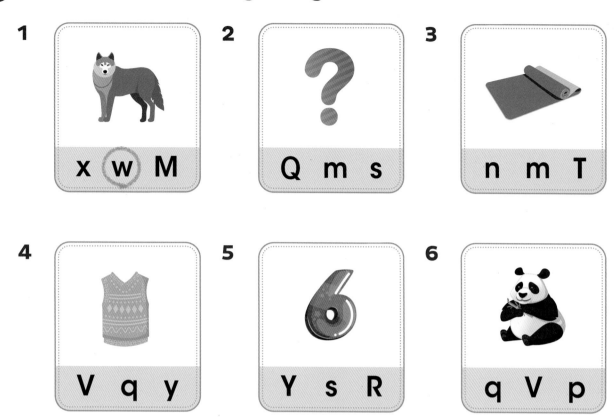

1 x (w) M

2 Q m s

3 n m T

4 V q y

5 Y s R

6 q V p

D Circle the pictures with the same beginning sound.

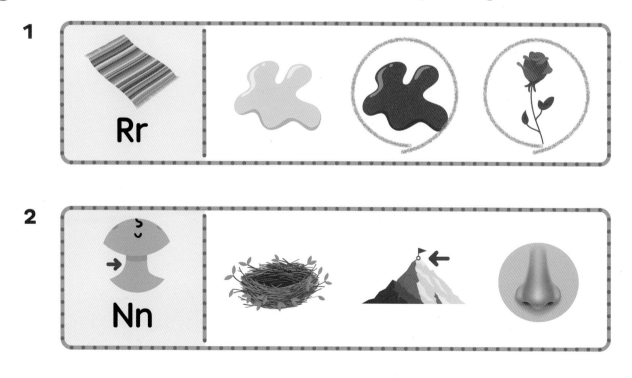

1 Rr

2 Nn

MEMO

MEMO

Oh! My Phonics is a four-level series of phonics books designed for EFL students to help them learn the fundamentals of phonics with efficient and practical methods. This series greatly assists young learners in understanding the relationship between letters and sounds effectively and adequately. *Oh! My Phonics* also introduces a number of common sight words embedded in fun phonics stories. In this way, children can naturally improve their sight word reading skills.

Oh! My Phonics Series

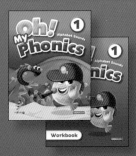

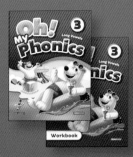

Alphabet Sounds

Short Vowels

Long Vowels

Double Letters

세이펜과 함께 배우는 Oh! My Phonics

⟨Oh! My Phonics⟩의 Student Book과 부록 플래시카드에는 세이펜이 적용되어 있습니다. 세이펜을 가져다 대기만 하면 원어민의 생생한 영어 발음과 억양을 듣고 영어 말하기 연습을 할 수 있습니다.

*번역 기능 | 세이펜으로 책을 찍어서 원어민 음성을 들은 후, ⓣ 버튼을 짧게 누르면 우리말 해석 음원을 들을 수 있습니다.

🖊 세이펜을 대면 Activity의 지시문을 들을 수 있습니다. ⓣ 기능 지원

🖊 유닛에서 배우게 될 글자에 세이펜을 대면 원어민의 정확한 발음을 들을 수 있습니다.

🖊 QR코드에 세이펜을 대면 해당 트랙의 MP3 파일이 재생됩니다.

🖊 각 단어나 그림에 세이펜을 대면 원어민의 정확한 발음과 억양을 들을 수 있습니다. ⓣ 기능 지원

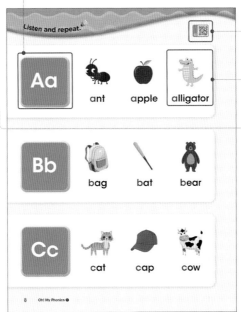

🖊 각 그림에 세이펜을 대면 원어민의 정확한 발음과 억양을 들을 수 있습니다. ⓣ 기능 지원

🖊 Listening 활동의 문제 번호에 펜을 대면 해당 문항의 음원이 재생됩니다.

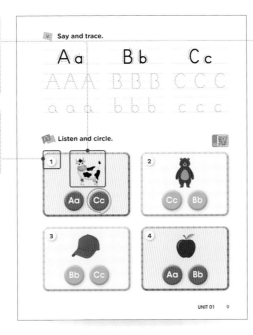

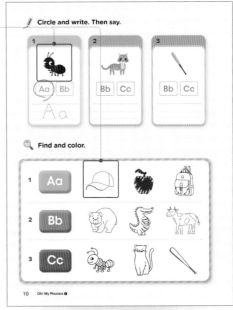

✏️ 각 단어나 그림에 세이펜을 대면 원어민의 정확한 발음과 억양을 들을 수 있습니다.
Ⓣ 기능 지원

✏️ 영어 문장에 세이펜을 대면 원어민의 정확한 발음과 억양을 들을 수 있습니다.
Ⓣ 기능 지원

✏️ 스토리에 등장한 각 Sight Word에 세이펜을 대면 원어민의 정확한 발음을 들을 수 있습니다.

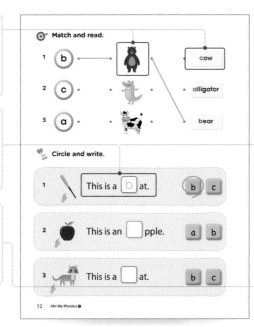

✏️ Listening 활동의 문제 번호에 펜을 대면 해당 문항의 음원이 재생됩니다.

✏️ 각 단어나 그림에 세이펜을 대면 원어민의 정확한 발음과 억양을 들을 수 있습니다.
Ⓣ 기능 지원

✏️ 각 글자에 세이펜을 대면 원어민의 정확한 발음을 들을 수 있습니다.

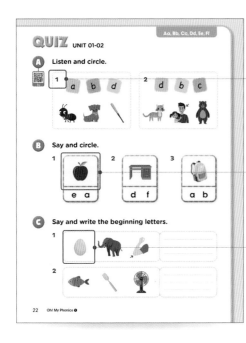

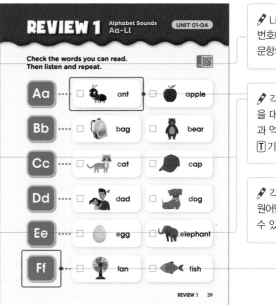

✏️ 플래시카드의 각 단어나 그림에 세이펜을 대면 원어민의 정확한 발음과 억양을 들을 수 있습니다.
Ⓣ 기능 지원

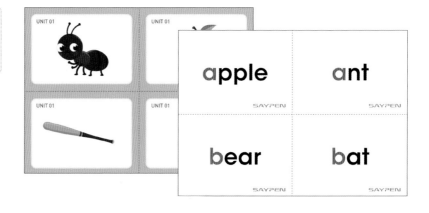